Seeds in tear-soaked soil

KATRINA JEFFS

Copyright © 2023 Katrina Jeffs
All rights reserved.
ISBN: 978 0 6459422 0 0

FOR LITTLE TRINA -

One day you will speak and they will listen.

Trigger warning: This book deals with themes of self-harm, suicide and eating disorders.

CONTENTS

	Dear Reader	i
PART 1	Buried	1
PART 2	Roots	33
PART 3	Blooms	75

DEAR READER

I grew up a quiet child, in the suburbs of south-west Sydney. I didn't speak much, but I loved to write. I remember spending weekends writing in my diary or writing short stories and I dreamt of seeing my name on the front of a book. Somewhere along the way, I lost the joy to perfectionism and the great creativity-killer – the need for praise.

In 2015, I was living alone, far from home. I thought my life was about to take off, instead, everything fell to pieces. In 2016, I was diagnosed with bipolar disorder, and anorexia nervosa soon followed. For the next few years I spent a lot of time in and out of hospital, in therapy and navigating the turbulent journey that is finding the right combination of medications. Thankfully, through all the pain, I picked up a pen again. I was no longer writing for praise; I wrote to survive – to spill my pain onto the page and get it out of my head. I wrote to try and make sense of what was happening to me. I wrote in hopelessness, in frustration and eventually, in hope. Even, eventually, with courage. This book is a collection of poetry and pieces that I wrote over the last eight years. Seeing them all compiled like this, looking back at how far I have come and sending my story out into the world, gives me the greatest feeling of pride that I have ever known and is incredibly therapeutic.

My road is still a winding one with many highs and lows but I am not the same person I once was. I thank you for reading this and hope that this book will make you feel something. Terror, despair, joy, hope… – I just hope you feel.

Many thanks to Chris Sowers and Dean Jeffs, without whom this book would never have existed.

Katrina

PART 1 - BURIED

Death must be so beautiful. To lie in the soft brown earth, with the grasses waving above one's head, and listen to silence. To have no yesterday, and no tomorrow. To forget time, to forgive life, to be at peace.
- Sylvia Plath

Seeds in tear-soaked soil

I

I stand in the pharmacy,
overwhelmed by brightly-coloured boxes,
facing a wall of medications
for chesty coughs
and hard flus
and spring hay fever
as I buzz from the surreal combination
of apathy and adrenaline.

Can I help you? she asks.
Not in the familiar, friendly way.
Her voice is laced with concern
and I wonder what part
of my body language
gave it away.
It could easily have been my heaving chest
or my shaking hands
or my sad, hollow eyes
and I want to scream at her -
Yes! Please help me!
Instead, I utter a blasphemous lie.
I'm okay.

But I am not oh-fucking-kay.
I am a lace curtain ripped roughly in half,
desperate to leave
but not ready to leap,
stuck between the peace of finality
and the panic of finality.
Head down,
hands in my hair,
I walk out and sob to the sky.
I am both relieved and devastated
to have missed another chance,
relieved and devastated to be living.

II

A strange fracturing in my perception,
a sudden shift that fills me
with that old, slow-burning panic.
All the life I have worked so hard to grow
I feel drain from my soul,
and I am left an empty shell.

Terrified.

III
Who is going
to love me
with this fucked up mind?

IV
I have looked in these mirrors,
seeing bones and feeling nothing
but dissatisfaction.
Is it really the feeling of thinness I crave,
or is it the feeling of fading away?
To silently fade away,
as I have always believed I was destined.
Silent, peripheral, ghostly.
It makes sense that I should want to take up as little space
as possible.
A whispering – fade away

fade away

fade away.

V

A spoonful of nothing
makes the numbers go down
and tastes like sugar-coated agony.
I disappear to survive,
I starve to live,
I count to stay.
I control to live another day.

Seeds in tear-soaked soil

VI

Useless

    fucking

        excuse

            for a

                human being.

VII

I watch vacantly as the water makes the blood slowly unfurl like orange smoke tendrils,
my mind experiencing a calm I've been longing for all day.
My arm throbs and stings in protest,
but the blade finds my skin again and again.
The pain that's been lodged and aching in my chest oozes hastily into the water and dissipates,
and I feel a quiet, familiar relief fall down upon me.
My skin lies stretched like a canvas with its red and smarting brushstrokes.
But this is no work of art.
It is merely a distraction from the turmoil within.

VIII
She has hidden all the knives in the house from me.
My medications are dispensed by her careful hand.
I have never felt more untrustworthy.
I have never felt more deranged.

IX
For such a good girl,
I've spent a lot of time in hell.

X

I have been told I am a mouse
by well-meaning nurses,
and I resented it.
They laugh as they unearth
my greatest of insecurities,
and I feel the urge to scuttle
into a tiny, dark hole
where I lick the wounds
life has brought upon me,
lamenting my weakness
and sniffing quietly,
as my wiry whiskers quiver.

XI

I am fragility.
I define it.
Like a glass I smash to the ground,
breaking into a million tiny pieces,
a small knock is all it takes.
It pains me to be this way,
to live life so cautiously for fear of shattering.
And when I do shatter, my god,
can't you hear the sound?
Shiny, sharp objects, ready to cut and make bleed,
flung here and there.
I know it is dangerous but please,
please stay.
I am tired.
If there is one thing I know,
it is that I have grown so tired
of gluing myself back together,
time and time again.

XII

Cover me with ivy of the deepest green,
let it stretch and twist its way
over this sickening body,
a body that I cannot bear to look at.
Let it pull tight at the soft edges
And envelop my limbs
until I grow verdant and lush
and become more living vine
than tainted blood and flesh.

XIII

If only we could bottle her blood!
I heard my teacher say.
No pride,
only downcast eyes and that same feeling
that plays over and over like a minor chord
throughout the song of my life.
I want to scream until my throat tears -

I am no angel!

And then whisper,
they don't live in hell.

Ten years later,
I shed that blood in a bathtub
wishing it would
all
drain
away.
The pedestal I had sat on was hard and high,
it made my knees shake
and I was tired, so tired,
of being good.
I sat away from the edge,
head on my knees,
wondering how I got here.
If only they knew,
they would order it all
to crumble to the ground
and leave me as colossal ruins.
Instead, they shone golden light onto me
and smiled as it scorched my skin.
They did not know,
they do not know,
that I am from a shadowy place,

dank, isolating, endless,
and that even if they had the Roman god Sol
do their bidding,
I would always return to the dark,
forever false gold.

XIV

I have stood,
shaking,
before that silky, black veil
that draws me near with promises
of peace and relief and rest,
and felt hopelessly,
desperately,
torn between the here and there.

XV

When even the shimmering stars
can't set my soul alight,
leave me in the deepest darkness
and let me drift to sleep.

XVI

Lifeless as a rose bush in the midst of winter,
I disappear once again to the dull, off-white corridors,
grey, dotted carpet and crispy, starched sheets.
I watch as the nurse writes 'unstable' on my paperwork,
I hesitate when she asks to see my arm.
A revolving door,
a ceaseless cycle,
yet another sojourn in this place where nurses and kitchen staff greet me by name
and where the too-sweet smell of soap turns my stomach.
The solitary hours merge hazily into days and into weeks as I haunt the halls,
lithium creeping through my veins.
Everything seems futile,
everything seems dark,
but in the midst of the tears and the purging and nails on skin,
I make a promise to myself –
I shall leave this place, blooming.

XVII
Can you keep yourself safe?
They question me over and over
and over again.
I say, all I could think of today
was my urge to buy pills.
Instead, I bought peonies.

Seeds in tear-soaked soil

XVIII
His eyes were the colour of earth
and like earth they could make me grow,
or they could bury me.

Seeds in tear-soaked soil

XIX
The ease in which your lies drip from your tongue,
disguised as honey but unveiled as acid,
breaks my trusting heart
every time.

XX

You'll find me in the old second-hand shop
amongst bone china antiques
and musty, leather-bound books,
tired and weathered and perishing,
propped up neatly on a shelf
with a small tag slung around my neck.
USED GIRL, it reads.

XXI

Where once protruded bone
now grows a snarling mound of flesh that swells and bulges
and rudely pushes its way out into the world.
The smudged change room mirror reflects a girl unable to breathe,
suffocated by too-tight clothes,
zips and buttons and seams politely trying to withstand the pressure that threatens to force them undone.
The betrayal of a body is a beastly thing.
Oh, gargantuan irony,
how cruel and heartless you are.
You have made a fool of me.
In horror I imagine barely stifled snickers echoing callously behind my back.
Look here, at the girl who longed to disappear.

XXII

Once upon a time my heart led the way to snow-capped mountains
and ancient castles
and cheap hostels
and late-night gelato,
my tongue stumbling unashamedly over foreign languages.
A quiet, determined gypsy-girl, travelling the world on a whim.
I long to be that girl again,
living free and open-hearted,
drunk on Kerouac rather than self-hate.

XXIII
Is this what dying feels like?
My consciousness slips quietly away
as the pills dissolve inside me.
I'm falling,
I'm falling,
into soft nothingness.
I float away from the world,
into peace.

XXIV

I think of my tiny nephews
and how I want them to know their aunty,
of how I do not want to be dead
before they have a memory of me,
but maybe that would be best.
Would it be worse if I were to die
when they will remember their melancholy aunt,
when they are strong enough to be her pall bearers?

XXV

I love Mother Nature,
she gives so much to me,
but never have I adored her more
than when I learnt of her suicide tree.

XXVI
When I leave,
grow garden roses from my grave.
They shall bloom and wither with the seasons,
like the tiresome comings and goings of my joy and sorrow.

XXVII
Why won't you just let me die?

XXVIII
I have sat,
fidgeting,
in a still room
with people wearing grave faces,
and felt the awkwardness
of nobody knowing
what to do with you
when you are mentally ill.
I don't blame them.
God knows,
I don't know what to do
with me, either.

XXIX

The graveyard lies amongst the trees,
beyond the church,
where the tolling bells have rattled
the bones of the dead
every fifteen minutes
for more than a hundred years.
I sit on the grave of some long-departed soul
and it occurs to me
that I will turn twenty-eight in two weeks.
On my birthday last year
my reflection was all bones
and sallow eyes.
I barely ate.
I was weak, dizzy, slowly dying.
Increased weight does not mean
increased contentedness,
but this birthday I will look at how far I have come,
and instead of seeing a body that takes up too much space,
I will see a body that survived.

XXX

This gentleness learnt to tie a noose.
This sweetness loves shards of glass.
This kindness wants me dead.
This gracefulness dreams of a bloody end.
You have not seen the horror scenes that exist
inside this sweeping cinematic drama.
If you look,
it will terrify you,
how things are very rarely
what they seem.

PART 2 – ROOTS

We shake with joy, we shake with grief.
What a time they have, these two
Housed as they are in the same body.
  - Mary Oliver

Seeds in tear-soaked soil

I
I see the soft, pink petals of the first camellia blooms,
a vision I hold with me all year,
and think – don't give up now.

II

Sarah says it is love.
I tell her it is obligation.
Sarah says it is love.
I tell her it is my fear of disappointing.
Sarah says it is love.
I tell her it is resentment.
Sarah says it is love.
I tell her it is oppression.
Sarah says it is love.
But I am spiteful and angry and bitter.
Sarah says it is love.
It is love that has kept me here.

III

The song I made plans to die to
was my favourite song when I was fourteen.
Alone in my room,
my chlorine-induced
premature rosacea cheeks
as pink as the lava lamp goo
moving noiselessly by my bed,
I'd put in the CD
and sing to the back of my eyelids,
not knowing that one day
I would choose this to be
the last thing I ever do.
It's all in how you mix the two,
but Blue and Yellow
make green,
and holiness and heaviness
make ghosts.

Seeds in tear-soaked soil

IV

Walls shut us in
to keep us safe
but when, like Alice,
you've outgrown the space,
the back of your neck against the ceiling,
you might find a way out
but that doesn't mean you're leaving.

Green and graffitied
were the cubicle walls
where I spent lunchtimes
hidden in my stall.
Silent, and ghost-like, not really there,
yet I didn't want a way out,
because I didn't belong there.

The bathroom
I bathed in as a child
shrunk to be something
more crimson, less pure and mild.
I forgot the turtle I splashed and made fly,
yet it's a hard thing to forget,
shedding your blood to survive.

The scales on the floor,
white gown on,
I'm still groggy
but I step on.
Numbers flash and then she says I can go,
as if I can go back to sleep with
the weight of those numbers in tow.

Grey, dotted carpet,
I know it well.
Actually, to be honest,

it reminds me of hell.
I've haunted those sterile halls,
I've collapsed to the floor,
I've pondered who would be the bearers of my pall.

Now, I'm far from home,
I've never seen these rooms,
yet there's something familiar…
I've been in these tombs.
Different rooms but the voices tell me I am nothing
I take too many drugs
just to feel something.

I'm sad in this room here,
frustrated and lost,
I had dreams to write and call it a life,
but it teases as a summer rose, always in frost.
I try but don't know what will make it bloom,
it seems each and every one,
will never be the right room.

V
CC:
Your heart can still be a beautiful place.

VI

This quiet gardener works away,
planting tiny seeds in many years' worth of deep, tear-soaked soil –
seeds of poetry and of prose and of art –
to see what life and beauty might grow from it.

VII

I have not slept for two weeks and my brain sizzles and sizzles like meat in a pan and I want to sleep but it does not happen because my brain has forgotten how to do it and I feel so stupid because it is always the same but I do not learn. The invincibility tricks me (what illness?) and then after so long with all that energy, I crash and feel less human than a lizard under a rock.

VIII

When someone treats me poorly
I see it as a reflection of my inadequacy.
If only I had been more giving,
more beautiful,
more outgoing,
happier,
more like someone else,
perhaps I would have been treated better.
As if being hurt by someone else isn't enough,
I hurt myself, too.
I blame myself.
This is one of the saddest realisations
I have had about myself.

IX

I live my life in the brace position,
always anticipating what comes next.
Will this be the crash that kills me?
I tense every muscle,
close my eyes tight,
ready for the sadness to sink into my cells
or the euphoria to fly me into chaos.

X

I know where the wild berries grow
Come, follow if you may
But heed my warning:
That fruit tastes sweet
Yet will all one day decay.

XI

Sometimes I am very, very sad
But sometimes I go to sleep thinking about cover illustrations
And knitted jumper colour combinations
And making hats for my cat's birthday celebrations
And on those nights,
I am grateful for the gentle reprieve.

XII
Nel nome del Padre...
I used to imagine the voice of my long-departed nonna
chanting as her fingertips danced over rosary beads,
and found comfort in the faith of my ancestors.
...e del Figlio...
Many years ago I knelt before an altar in the red city of Bologna,
silently pleading for my misery to be taken away
but heard only the polite footsteps of whispering tourists
on the ancient marble floor.
...e dello Spirito Santo...
Recently I stood sobbing on a beach in front of fellow mourners,
poetry tumbling roughly from my mouth like the waves,
hot, burning injustice growing in my chest and forcing tears
to swim in my eyes.
Nel nome del Padre...
For I had spent weeks crying and pleading with the heavens –
if a soul must be taken,
God, just let it be mine.
...e del Figlio...
This soul that unashamedly craves the stillness of the grave,
so shockingly ungrateful and flippant about life's joy,
was offering itself up as an exchange.
...e dello Spirito Santo.
Amen.

Today on a hospital form I found the familiar tick-a-box to
identify religion,
determining the faith of the man who would come hurrying
through the sterile hallways
should things not go as planned.
Nel nome del Padre...
With my pencil hovering briefly for the first time in my life,

I made a small mark in the box that read:
Atheist.
...e del Figlio...
It should have been me.
...e dello Spirito Santo...
God, it should have been me.
Amen

XIII

It has caused me so much grief,
believing that I must be one thing or the other.
I am the rose that grows, soft and gentle,
in the garden,
and I am the rose dropped in the midst of sorrow,
into the grave.

XIV

I will wait for you here,
in this soft dappled sunlight
beneath the dancing leaves,
autumn air chilling my cheeks.
Or perhaps
I will have to wait for you with heavy eyes
on a swamped peak hour train ride,
aching to be home.
Nevertheless I will wait for you here,
in this universe,
and I will wait for you in any other.
I will wait for you.

XV

He talks of beauty with such assurance
that I feel he could believe any absurd, impossible thing.
I think he might start to believe that ripe round oranges are dug up from the warm earth by tired farmers with sun-stained, leather hands
and that tiny, striped kittens hazard their first squeaks in nests high atop the trees
and that a silver star could fall right into the palm of his outstretched hand on a dark and quiet night.
He talks of beauty as though I should believe it, too,
as though to me it is not comparable to prehistoric beasts walking among us,
showing their teeth when they say, startled,
"what do you mean we're not supposed to be here?"

XVI

If I boldly showed you the thin, white scars that crisscross messily on my arm like the underside of an embroidery piece,
if I recounted tales of too many pills and how they made me swagger and sway through the early morning dark,
if I read to you from that old diary, full of desperation and hopes for death, written in a lonely hospital room,
if I shared my shame at having sought my worth in warm but ill-fitting arms,
tell me,
would you stay?
When I lay down at your feet the shadowy past of some other girl,
will you wonder how I came to carry it?
If I allowed you to know the cold and bitter pain that is unreconcilable with the flowers and the sunshine that you've come to know,
tell me,
would you stay?

XVII

It was midnight and we wandered slowly through the quiet streets as golden light sleepily crawled through stained-glass windows and rested on the footpath where we swayed and twirled to that Ed Sheeran song and I spied the lemon tree in someone's yard and exalted as I picked a bulbous piece of yellow fruit to hold to my nose and breathe in its fresh scent while you filled my ears with warm murmurings of sweetness and beauty and caught me more than once as I tripped over wayward concrete and I hugged you tight and felt safe in your arms as we made our way home at midnight in the cool spring breeze.

Seeds in tear-soaked soil

XVIII

When I said "I love you", I meant that loving you feels like seven years ago when I stood on the side of the highway late at night, drinking in the vast, starry sky. The universe flowed slowly over my tongue and settled gently in my chest, the stars flickering around my tired heart and forming dazzling new constellations within me. I stood, transfixed, in the lonely, impenetrable darkness, not understanding why the universe would choose me as its home but raising my palms upwards in gratitude nonetheless. What I meant to say, amor, is that my love for you feels like encountering the immensity of the cosmos on the outskirts of a quiet outback town. I cannot explain it with three short words or some grand, overreaching metaphor. I just meant that when the universe turned inside me on that warm spring night, I felt the rare and reassuring peace of knowing that, somehow, all is as it should be. All is as it should be.

XIX

Mi amor,
you are in the first glorious sip of tea on a winter afternoon,
when the sun warms gently and makes shadows stretch
lazily across these suburban lawns.
You are in the sweet, woody scent that hides, shyly,
between the pages of my books.
You are in the pretty, pastel colours of a tranquil sunset,
painted by an artist who carefully positions you between
warm tangerines,
fairy floss pinks
and quiet lavenders.
You are in the steady, glowing fire that crackles in the
hearth,
enticing people near and giving them warmth,
and sleep,
and comfort.
My dear,
you are in all that comforts me, or gifts me joy,
or calms this wild and grateful heart.

XX

My mother says
that when she held me
in her arms
for the first time,
she felt a love like no other.
The kind of love
that changes everything.
The kind of love
that makes hearts full,
that makes tears of joy
cascade from eyes,
and brings new meaning
and purpose to life.
I am terribly fearful that one day
I will hold my own child
in my arms
and feel that surge of love,
the elation and the hope
for this precious,
fragile new life,
a life that depends on me
and yet,

I will still want to die.

XXI
I have seen a delicate fern growing out of concrete and thought –
Why shouldn't I, too, grow from a hard and difficult place?

XXII

You were meant to hear the heavy tumbling of the rhythmic, unrelenting waves,
and feel it move oceans within you.
You were meant to amble under the dappled shade of tall, quiet trees,
who have observed patiently for generations those that pass below their leaves.
You were meant to gaze up at the universe, its velvet black expanse sparkling silently above,
and wonder if it gazes back at you.
You were meant to breathe in the crisp, smoky mountain air,
feeling it chill your cheeks,
and fill your heart,
and unfurl long-ago memories within you.
While you stare for hours into a small, illuminated screen,
searching for connection but finding discontent
and shame
and envy,
know that there is a whole world out there,
offering connection for the lonely,
wonder for the apathetic
hope for the hopeless.
Go lightly, seek yourself in the world.

XXIII
I was a thing of no substance,
hollow and silent,
and I hated myself for it.
Now, I send spontaneous words
across rooms full of people
who have no idea that
in that moment I feel strong
and brave
and new
and grown
but just count the seconds
until my own fists fly,
beating me up
for daring to speak
until I am bruised all over
and I hate myself still.
I grow and I grow
and it hurts
and I grow.
I once stood back,
shy and ghost-like,
and despised myself for it.
Now I start conversations,
make jokes,
laugh loudly,
but nobody knows
that the rest of the day
is spent keeled over in agony
in a familiar, dark corner of my mind,
where I am told I am too much,
an embarrassment,
shameful -
"Who do you think you are?"
and I despise myself still.
I grow and I grow

Seeds in tear-soaked soil

and it hurts
and I grow
but at least I am growing
and one day,
perhaps,
I will speak without flinching,
take up space without ducking,
and simply exist without anticipating pain.

XXIV

This time last year
I was in a dark room
with three burning candles
and a question.
I asked it to the darkness
with a heart of lead,
to three who are gone,
three who are dead.
The flames hardly moved
in the breathless room,
I cried without sound
and waited.
The fire disappeared
into wisps of smoke,
and in nineteen days
from a dream I woke.
We are gone, he said,
but it's not your time
you must stay - please stay,
dear granddaughter of mine.

XXV

When I was five
I was told not to run
towards the playground.
I ran anyway,
stopped abruptly by a fall
that lodged a shard of glass
into my knee.
I remember the blood that oozed
and I was left with an inch-long scar
to remind me of the time
that I felt that sting while
running joyfully towards something.
I have other scars,
also made by sharp slithers of glass,
but I did not feel that sting
from falling to the ground,
but falling to pieces.
I was not running towards something
but away.
I only wanted to escape.

Seeds in tear-soaked soil

XXVI

Unknown hands etched the scars into the tree,
but the ones on my arm were etched by me.
The tree still grows
and so do I,
symbols to reflect on
and then walk on by.

XXVII

There are deep scratches
on the dark floorboards
that lead to Death's door,
and I made them.
I will admit,
sometimes I have crawled,
exhausted,
but willing and ready,
only to turn back
before knocking at the portal
between the here and there,
and to be honest,
I still don't know why.
Other times Death has dragged me
roughly by the feet
towards the door, snarling,
'enough is enough!'
And although I would have liked to end
the struggle right then,
I fought,
dug deep into that most ancient of wood
with my nails until they broke and bled.

And I stayed.

I've never been interested in making pretty,
buffing those floorboards
until they were smooth and gleaming,
until there was no trace
of my fight,
as though I had never been there at all.
I know I'll be back there some time,
with more splinters lodged in my fingertips.
And really,
I prefer that others know

Seeds in tear-soaked soil

the kind of person they are dealing with.
There are some of us among the living
who already know the scent
that fills the room
with a sweep of Death's cloak.
For me,
it's never something rancid and awful,
but something comforting,
warm,
like a cup of tea made just how I like,
and sweet cinnamon cookies,
and the promise of no more pain,
and to resist it all
is to possess strength unknown,
strength not understood,
unless you, too,
have heard those floorboards creak underfoot.

XXVIII

We are fed the lie that 'happy' is our default state and so if we are not happy, we are doing something wrong. We are failing in some way. Yet human beings are made to experience a huge range of emotions. I know what it is like to be the sad person in the room, to feel miserable for feeling miserable. My sense of worthlessness was all-consuming. I thought I was a failure when, in fact, I was human. Life is hard and gritty and heartbreaking <u>as well as</u> fulfilling and joyful and beautiful. Teach this to your children and remember, no feeling is final.

XXIX

You hear her calling out to you,
not like a mother shouting for her children to come in for tea,
but gently
warmly
patiently
with arms ready to embrace.
You see,
she's noticed the signs.
A body that can never get enough sleep.
The emptiness in your grey eyes.
The constant overwhelm
and the usual thoughts.
I just can't do life.
The Forest knows.
As you heed her call
and walk deep into the wilderness
you think about the conversations happening under your feet.
The trees chatter a lot,
did you know?
The water chills your feet until they burn,
the bell birds ring out of sight,
you marvel at ancient rock formations,
and as you leave,
you place your hand on the smooth, white bark of an old ghost gum and whisper -
thank you.
Mother always knows.

XXX

I turned away from my wide horizon,
travelled the 600 kilometres home,
and now it's been eight years
since I made you proud.
Held up by two sturdy pillars,
when I should be able to walk on my own,
my shame and wounded pride
are hidden by the ugly mask of ingratitude.
It pains me that I am still here,
so far behind my peers.
For twenty-five years
I was going somewhere
until the tracks froze over
and the jarring halt left me
suspended in mid-air,
suspended in time,
caught in a liminal state
where both my past and a future
were unreachable.
I clawed at the air
but all was still.

XXXI

I tell myself,
I tell others,
I'll stay for one more winter.
I'll see how things go.
I am not promising anything.
Then I stay the winter
and I tell them,
just three more months.
I'll let the spring decide.
Summer arrives and I tell them,
I'll endure this heat and see.
And then it is autumn,
I watch things die
and I wait to see if I will.
I wait,
and I wait,
I stay,
and I stay.
One small bit at a time.
This is how I stay.

XXXII

When I have wandered through cemeteries
searching for meaning in crumbling tombstones and fading epitaphs,
in a healthy strawberry plant that grows from earth filled with death,
not knowing that my DNA lay under my feet -
did my ancestors move inside their graves?
Did their bones sing out to me?
Did the dust within their coffins swirl and say with loving earnestness,
"My child, memento mori!"
"My child, memento mori!"

XXXIII

Sweet raspberry juice stains my cheeks like gentle war paint
And I am reunited with mother moon.
Within the earth things twist and creep
Ready as am I
Yet mother moon looks down to say
Soon, darlings, soon.

XXXIV

A tired young woman dropped a small seed into a pot of soil.
She had kept the seed while making orange juice.
The woman covered the seed, patted the soil and poured a little water on top.
She did this even though she felt very sad.
She often felt sad.
Sometimes she felt so sad that she wanted to disappear.
Other times, she felt so joyful and bubbly
that she thought she might explode into a cloud of colourful confetti.
Often the woman felt not **so** sad and not **so** bubbly
but she wasn't sure what to call this in-between feeling.
When the sadness filled her up,
her hope vanished.
She had wondered in the early morning hours
and while strolling on sunny days,
while driving in her car
and while sipping chai in cafes,
what she could do to *make hope stay*.
Even just a **tiny** bit.
When she had looked at that smooth orange seed,
she'd had an idea.
So she dropped the seed into the soil
but she poured in her tiny hope as well.
She *hoped* to grow old enough to see the seed become a tree,
to plant it in a yard of her own
and to have children that she could pick oranges
and sip fresh, sweet juice with.
Through many nights and days,
the pot with the seed sat quietly.
The woman gave it some water every day
and spent a lot of time gazing at the dirt,
allowing herself to dream.
One morning, she spotted something green.

Seeds in tear-soaked soil

The orange tree was growing!
And her hope was growing with it.
She knew it because she could feel it in her heart.
Months passed.
The sadness visited to try and steal her hope
and the confetti also stopped by,
making a lot of mess.
The seed and her hope just kept growing slowly through it all.
Each new leaf was a celebration.
She could see the children running wildly on the grass
and could almost feel the smooth surface of an orange in the palm of her hand
as she pushed and twisted to make juice.
Today, the small tree is twenty centimetres tall and has sixteen shiny leaves.
The growth of hope is not as easy to measure as a tree,
but the woman could feel it moving in her heart…

She sits silently and watches the tree.
She hopes that when it is much taller and stronger,
she will be here to take another seed,
and with the help of her children,
bury it carefully in some soil.
And she would pour in new hope.
Hope to see her children grow up,
to teach them about joy and sorrow
and to see her hair turn white.

XXXV

I am not me,
not who I was,
I have never known this person before.
I don't know who you see,
it's not who I was,
I'm waxing and waning at my core.
When did the mouse
become a wolf,
standing tall to howl at the moon?
Or is it a guise
and this wolf that you see,
shall be stripped of its costume soon?
I despised the mouse
but I hate the wolf,
for the latter I do not trust.
It howls instinctively
but this causes pain,
I'm left whimpering with face flushed.
I am not me,
not who I was,
I was fragile and hateful and shy.
So am I the mouse
or am I the wolf?
Upon which should I rely?

XXXVI

I watched my mother sleeping,
the day that marked forty-one years
since her mother died.
Three generations of women,
from one country to another,
all connected by the womb.
What have we in common
other than blood and soul?
The curse of goodness –
to be good at all costs,
and I know in my bones
that this curse
lies with me to break.

PART 3 – BLOOMS

I hope you will go out and let stories, that is life, happen to you, and that you will work with these stories...water them with your blood and tears and your laughter till they bloom, till you yourself burst into bloom.
- Clarissa Pinkola Estés

Seeds in tear-soaked soil

I
I crave purpose
once again,
a way to earn
and a way
to be worthy,
instead of feeling lost
in the most vast of moors,
all my faults
and my past exposed
to the wide open sky,
no sense of direction.
All I know is that
underneath trees that reach
high above me,
or with my hands in the dirt,
or catching the scent
of wood smoke
or seeing a shoot grow from seed,
there is no worthy
or unworthy,
no failure,
not a sense of being lost,
but indeed a sense of being home,
and shouldn't that be enough?
Isn't that enough?

Seeds in tear-soaked soil

II

To as far back
as my memory goes,
a single new flower was tied each week
to the fence that was installed on the bridge
to prevent it from happening again.
But then months followed months,
and the same flower stayed there,
wrapped in plastic,
but brittle and dead.
Each time I crossed that bridge
I wondered if the people
who were left to remember
were gone, too.
Did anybody else notice
that sad, decaying rose,
as they went about their day?
Was I the only one to grieve
for this person I did not know?
Did anybody else drive over that bridge,
wondering what it would be like
to jump off it?
All that cold, hard bitumen
and busy traffic
underneath them?

III

The community garden
felt much like a cemetery,
with bits of earth
organised into numbered plots
that we paid for
to bury things.
Perhaps they really aren't so different,
for life grows from death
and death grows from life
and this is how the world
has always worked.
Whether we sit by the grave
or sit by the plot,
we are sitting with death
as well as
the magic that grows from it.

IV
All of the flowers
cannot bloom at one time.
We must watch the snow bells decay
if we wish to marvel
at the summer roses.

V

You exist because of thousands of years of circumstances and choices made by your ancestors. If just one moment had happened differently in any of their lives – a change of mind, a minute of lateness, the weather on a certain day, a sudden emotion – history would have altered its course even just a tiny bit and therefore, you would not be here. You are a link in an incredibly intricate chain of lives, all connected no matter how distant they are. Remember this when you are lonely or hurting or feeling worthless. Your ancestors felt this, too. Search for their stories. Let them give you strength.

VI

I am a child of my ancestors,
birthed by my mother,
created by thousands of beating hearts
that pumped blood as red as my own,
that beat across centuries and faraway lands
where words fall strangely off the tongue
and where old folktales are sent
like whispers on the wind
across wide, treacherous seas,
always calling me home,
calling me home.

VII

You, the last of your generation,
paint pictures for us of worlds
that we will never know.
They float like dreamscapes
before our eyes -
a small country town,
a rabbit trapper,
an old cottage with too many kids.
A staunch Catholic,
a dirt road,
hunger and handmade things.
Your brothers are buried,
your sisters are too,
your parents left long ago.
I heard that dying slowly
is dying lonely,
but please know,
you are not alone.
We might be young
and paint with different colours
but we long to see your art.
We will walk with you
while you still can
and sketch your pictures
on our hearts.

VIII

I felt proud of myself
when I intuitively turned the sparkling, dying embers into
dancing flames.
The knowledge is in my bones,
my ancestors did it for thousands of years,
to survive.
And then I wonder why I am more proud
to set something alight
than I am for bringing myself back to life
from fading ashes,
time and time and time again.
It's not a small thing,
to set fire to a cold heart.
But then, as humans,
it's what we do, isn't it?
It's etched into our bones,
our ancestors did it for thousands of years,
to survive.

IX

My mother told me
that one day, while making the bed,
she had asked her mother –
how do you know if someone is the One?
In her thick Italian accent she simply replied –
when you know, you know.
I thought of this in that old café.
I did not wake up on that day
knowing that I was going to ask
such a big question,
but there, staying warm
from the cold outside,
I took his hand.
I uttered those words
that I had believed
I was not meant
to hear
or to say.
But there he was,
and there I was,
without caution or fear,
and I wondered if this if what Nonna meant,
this feeling of knowing,
this feeling of courage,
this feeling that after all the shocking mess,
it would finally,
all become clear.

X

I see her by the fire,
with grey hair
and her knitting in her lap.
She is quiet
and pensive
and tired
and proud,
proud because she is me.
I never imagined myself
as an old woman
until some weeks ago,
and when I realised this,
it was a sad blow -
to think that I have always believed
I would be dead
long before my hair had the chance
to turn grey.
But I see her now,
and this must be progress.
I scream in the face
of a society ruled by a media
that says we must stay young -
I want the silver hair
and a creased face,
the niggling aches
that slow my pace,
the stories
and the wisdom
and all the heartbreak
that wisdom grows from.
What a privilege to have made it,
to have survived it all,
to do what I once deemed to be
entirely impossible.
To deny Death,

Seeds in tear-soaked soil

delay the grave,
and to see my hair turn grey.

XI
Outside,
things I have buried
to ease my sorrow
move in the earth
as the soft, grey sky
sheds tears over them
and shouts about things
not always needing
to be sunny,
for anyone who will listen.
Inside,
black velvet.
Crimson nails dance over
flour and knives and dark chocolate,
casting spells that fill the kitchen
with the scents of brownies
and chai
and drying oranges.
I sing Taylor's folklore
and dream of tiny, chubby hands,
the woods,
and stillness,
and find myself saying,
as within,
so without,
as without,
so within.

XII

On this slow night,
this winter solstice,
the darkness falls heavily
and lays long over all living things
while they wait for the sun
and warmth to return.
Just as I have sat in the blackest of shadows
lamenting that I would never see light again,
it returns anyway.
It rises steadily over the horizon
and at those magnificent times
and on this night,
we must look inside
and ask ourselves -
what do I want to leave behind in the darkness?
And what shall I bring with me into the light?

XIII

Two years,
two men,
my softness mauled,
torn apart like playdough
in their wide, sun-tanned hands.
The first shattered my spirit into pieces
and, instead of giving up,
I embarked on the messy job of
taking glue to the parts of myself
that I could salvage.
I sat in the old second-hand shop,
used and thrown away
like the weathered suitcases
and chipped plates around me
until someone else saw my cracks
and licked his lips at my weakness,
taking me for himself,
and I had hope.
Shame can make you sick
but I did not know it
until it rose up angrily inside me,
splattered aggressively onto the white porcelain of the bath,
the stinging taste of bile in my mouth,
tears falling from my eyes.
Is it abuse if you play along,
too afraid to say no?
I wonder how many women
throughout history
have asked themselves the same.
Some would call me a victim,
others would condemn me,
but I have given up
drawing my own blood
to punish myself for things
of which I am not guilty.

Seeds in tear-soaked soil

They call me a witch now
and I sit on my throne of bones
with cracked parts of myself healed
that I never thought could be
and I did it my goddamned self.
I keep a rhododendron branch
carefully placed across my lap,
and I am no longer afraid.
Things with healed scars
are often the fiercest,
for they have felt the pain
and seen it through,
and I am not afraid.
I am not afraid
to say
no.

XIV

I sit alone in the dark
by the light of a candle
and whisper to the wall -

I'm going to die.
I'm going to die.

I feel no sorrow
and I feel no fear,
only my soul shaking my bones,
like a prisoner in a cage,
who screams through the bars

I'm alive!
I'm alive!

I must live while I survive!

Seeds in tear-soaked soil

XV
I study sadness,
delve into what disturbs,
knead the nervousness
and dissect the depression.
I am a scholar of my own darkness.

XVI
Secret wishes scatter dandelion seeds
and deepest grief plants a remembrance rose.
Nostalgia grows the pansies of your childhood winters
and love grows zinnias because they remind you of her.
Hope digs daffodil bulbs into the autumn earth
and patience tends to a tree.
A garden grows from more than seeds and toil.
A garden grows from more than water and soil.

XVII

If it could've been you,
it would've been you.
Do you ever look back
at the path you did not take
because the brambles frightened you?
Have you realised now
that a lush garden waited just beyond,
if only you'd gone through?

XVIII

Do not dare to tell me sagely
about someone you know
who rebounded from rock-bottom
as though I did not smash through it
and crawl back up again with bloody hands
to turn my life around.
I made it and this is as good as it gets,
living life as a slot machine -
just insert pills to start.
Lights glow from within
the dark caverns in my eyes,
but will snuff out savagely
when the machine is deprived.
The game is rigged
and the prize is a lie
but it's something to do,
isn't it?
I am still sat here playing day after day,
eating pills and slapping buttons,
it's what I have to do.
It might not seem like much to you
but just look at my scarred hands.
It was a hard-fought battle
and my blood is still dripping
down the walls I had to climb.
So do not speak to me about rock-bottom
or turning my life around.
From where I've been,
I've never been further,
and the weather is quite good here.
I'm building a fire,
I'm pitching a tent,
and between two trees
I'm stringing up a washing line.

XIX

There is dirt clinging to my slippers
because I rose early from sleep
and fled noiselessly to the garden
while the lorikeets were still busy in the camellias
and the bees had not yet begun
humming their old working song.

XX

I had a vivid dream one restless night,
when my head ached and ached,
that I built my home within the walls
of the house of Emily Dickinson.
Hunting for some hidden meaning
beneath this strange but tangible vision,
I unearthed a box within which I found
a handed-down sense of safety,
an intricately crafted piece of needlework
and an old, used sword that I took up
and finally felt brave.
It was then that I felt writing calling to me,
once again,
as it did when I was a child,
sitting in my room,
scrawling stories on Saturday mornings
not for some tattered pieces of praise
that soon perish,
but for the satisfaction of spilling my soul
onto the page in the form of words.

XXI

Within the walls of the stone church
a dream unfolded like parchment paper
that I almost threw into the fire,
thinking it was destined to be ash.
Adorned with rich, burgundy velvet,
neatly embroidered with roses,
my grandmother's gold Christening brooch
pinned to my chest,
I grinned as I walked down the aisle
to my secret song
and met the man who loves me.
He loves me.
He loves me.
I have needed to put it down in ink to remind myself,
because after a lifetime of covertly reading minds
and seeing only dislike in bold, clickbait type,
I must read something true.
I tarnish golden people
with that same old brush I have used
for awkward encounters at too-loud parties,
where my quietness and my past feel ridiculous.
The day the autumn leaves sprawled
over that old stone
and he and I walked with cold hands entwined into the afternoon,
I buried that piece of parchment paper
in a secret place
so that I might unfold it again
and again
and again
and relive the day when I truly read nothing,
only listened,
and heard.
He loves me.

XXII

I am not afraid of Death
because he is an old friend of mine.
We've had our squabbles,
he and I,
we've danced together,
he's seen me cry,
he has given me solace
through the hardest of times.
Every day,
I think of him,
I remember my old friend,
and because I know him,
I am not scared
to meet him at the end.

XXIII

You may come to me sad
or lonely
or elated
or angry
or depleted
or anxious
or excited
or fed up.
Come to me as you are,
and I shall give your heart the space it needs
to feel its ever-changing and natural range of emotions.
Raw, honest vibes only.

XXIV

When I bury a seed,
I bury hope,
a hope more tiny
than the seed itself.
Barely there.
Yet from the barren soil,
by the most mysterious magic,
life grows,
and with it,
hope.
Mesmerised,
I wait for tomorrow,
and then I stay for the spring.

Seeds in tear-soaked soil

XXV
My life does not make sense
anywhere beyond the garden.
The garden is the only place
where dying and blooming
and dying and blooming
is something of beauty
and so I flee from the world
to the dirt -
to where I know I belong.

ABOUT THE AUTHOR

Katrina Jeffs lives in Sydney, Australia. She is a primary school teacher, gardener and writer who loves cats, cemeteries and anything old.

www.ingramcontent.com/pod-product-compliance
Lightning Source LLC
Chambersburg PA
CBHW022019290426
44109CB00015B/1232